LIMERICK RUN LACES

AN INTRODUCTION

PAT EARNSHAW

GORSE PUBLICATIONS · GUILDFORD

LIMERICK RUN LACES: AN INTRODUCTION

Machine nets decorated simply by running a blunt-tipped needle in and out of the meshes were the most successful of the various embroidered laces that were first established in the city of Limerick, in southern Ireland, in 1829.

Hampered for several decades by inadequate design, but bolstered by the lively capacity of the lacemakers for inventing stitches, the industry reached its aesthetic flowering during the prosperous days of the mid-1880s, and its greatest commercial success between then and the outbreak of war in 1914.

This book is based on three examples of Limerick lace from this period. It describes the materials used, the setting up of the work, and the various stitches of the solid and decorative areas, thus pointing the way for Limerick run laces to be recreated as closely as possible to their original form.

British Library Cataloguing-in-Publication Data

A catalogue record for this book is available from the British Library

ISBN 0 9513891 6 5

© Pat Earnshaw 1992

Printed by Staples Printers Rochester Ltd, Rochester, Kent ME2 4LT

Typeset by Alastair Thompson, Paris, France
in Helvetica and Avant Garde

for Gorse Publications, PO Box 214,
Shamley Green, Guildford GU5 0SW,
England

By the same author:

The Identification of Lace
A Dictionary of Lace
Bobbin and Needle Laces, Identification and Care
Lace in Fashion from the Sixteenth to the Twentieth Centuries
Lace Machines and Machine Laces
Needle-made Laces
Youghal and other Irish Laces
Youghal Lace, the Craft and the Cream
Threads of Lace from Source to Sink
Embroidery Skills: Needlelace
Outlines and Stitches, a Guide to Design, with special reference to Halas
   Needle Laces

ORIGINS OF LIMERICK LACE

Limerick laces are hand embroideries on machine net.

Their manufacture was introduced into Ireland by Charles Walker, in 1829.

Embroidered net industries had already existed in England for at least a decade. In Nottingham, a running stitch was used, the sewing needle being taken in a ducking manner in and out of the meshes of the net. In Coggeshall, the decoration was by means of a chain stitch, worked not with a needle but with a tambour hook which could be manipulated at great speed.

The twenty-four Englishwomen who accompanied Walker to Ireland were skilled in both techniques, and a flourishing workshop was rapidly estabished. Hundreds of embroiderers were soon employed, and later well over a thousand.

The work spread to many centres in Ireland, notably Kinsale, Cork, Dublin and even Newry in County Down. But regardless of where the lace was actually made it was still called 'Limerick', to emphasize that the basic technique remained constant. Such indeed is the normal practise with lace names: Honiton lace for example was made extensively at nearby Beer, and also at several centres in Ireland; while the Convent of Kenmare housed an important school of design for Youghal laces, as well as a very professional set-up for their manufacture.

The inevitable fluctuations of fashion, combined with the rigid conformity demanded by each change, reinforced the familiar industrial alternation of over-production and slump, making it impossible for the output of Limerick lace to follow a smoothly climbing curve. In fact, for nearly thirty years in the mid-century, additional factors, such as inefficient marketing, lack of training, inadequate attention to the quality of the work, and insufficient nous on the part of the supervisors to appreciate the overwhelming importance in commerce of attractive design, conspired to demote both the desirability and saleability of the work.

A splendid revival at the end of the nineteenth century coincided with the spendthrift opulence of the belle époque, and some of the most beautiful examples of Limerick run date from this time. But the outbreak of war in 1914, followed by disruptive social upheavals and then by partition in 1921, put an end to any economic possibility of paying a living wage for the hundreds of hours required by the embroiderers to produce substantial and perfect pieces.

This book concentrates on Limerick run laces, and is an introduction to their making.

The essential materials are simple: machine net, needles, thread, a pattern. Small pieces can be carried around and worked in odd moments.

Instructions are given for setting up the work, for embroidering the solid design areas, and for a number of decorative stitches.

The stitches and designs, taken from antique laces in the author's collection, are illustrated by photographs showing the final appearance of the lace. In addition, the working of each stitch is explained in written instructions and by line drawings.

THE PARTS OF A LACE

For convenience of study, lace fabrics can be distinguished into three distinct areas:

solid, decorative, openwork

The form taken by each area varies according to the technique and origin of the lace, but is constant for any particular type, and so a great help in identification.

In this example, the areas of a Limerick run lace are indicated by letters. For (B) a limited range of alternative stitches can be used.

Here, a special outline thread is used to define the caskets, but not the solid areas.

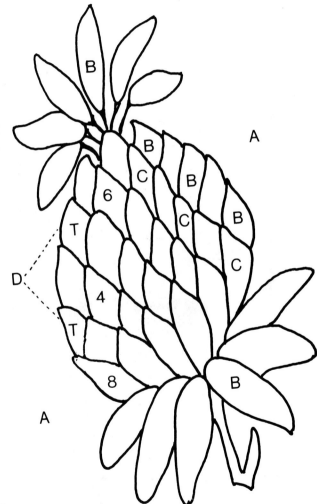

A fragment of a Limerick run sampler
A = openwork ground (machine net)
B = solid design areas (closely compacted running stitch)
C = caskets filled with decorative stitches
D = outline thread - used here only around the caskets
T = tent stitch
nos. 4, 6, 8 = casket stitches (seepp.42-45)

3

MATERIALS

Net

Plain cotton bobbinet is available in three mesh sizes, expressed as the number of meshes per inch (or other unit) measured horizontally.

Bobbinet is also known as twist net, because of the way it is constructed. The meshes are hexagonal, each side being made by the interaction of two net threads. On four of the sides the threads are twisted twice around each other, while on the sides which occupy the top and bottom positions during manufacture they cross over.

In old Limerick laces, a different type of net was most often used. The mesh shape was not hexagonal (round) but diamond-shaped (square). The four sides were elongated by additional twists while the cross sides were so severely shortened as to be scarcely visible.

Unfortunately, square nets went out of production during the 1960s, and though most of the traditional stitches can be worked equally well on the round net, they do not always look entirely the same.

Raschel nets, made by a warp-knitting process and using synthetic thread, can be used instead of cotton bobbinet. They are less expensive, available in a number of colours, and have a greater variety of mesh sizes. Synthetic threads should be used to embroider them since the mesh sides may cut through cotton.

Two-twist (round)   Four-twist (square)

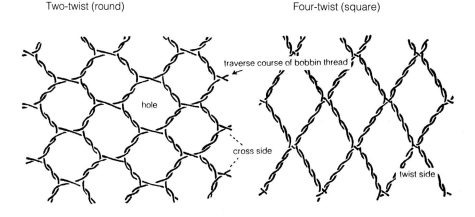

traverse course of bobbin thread

hole

cross side

twist side

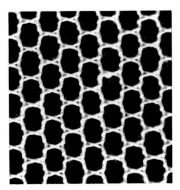 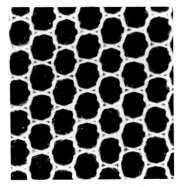 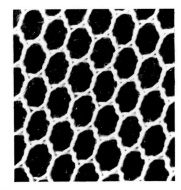

Round bobbinets with 15, 17 and 19 meshes per inch, measured over the cross sides.

Supports and patterns

The threads of the net run transversely, making it stretchable. To preserve the shape of the lace during working, sew the net to the pattern with tacking stitches, preferably worked in a different colour to avoid confusion with the stitches of the lace.

If the design involves a large number of different stitches, number these on the pattern for ease of reference.

If larger pieces of lace are attempted - a veil or flounce for example - a wooden embroidery frame with a roller to take up the worked piece helps to keep the net smooth and uncrumpled. Again tack the paper pattern beneath the net. All tacking stitches must be kept well away from the design area to prevent any conflict of threads.

If the design involves repeating a leaf or a sprig over and over again, the pattern for this need only be drawn once, and then moved on from one part of the net to the next as each outline is completed.

A simple motif has been drawn in waterproof ink on a backing of coloured self-adhesive paper, which can be stuck on to a card. Number the stitches, and tack the net over the pattern.

Outline of leaf run in   Pattern moved to next position

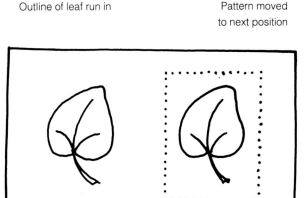

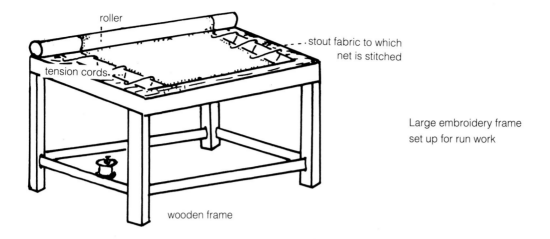

roller

stout fabric to which
net is stitched

tension cords.

wooden frame

Large embroidery frame
set up for run work

It is also possible to draw the pattern in pencil or in water-soluble ink directly on to the net. You may find this easier than attaching and detaching a separate pattern, but it does mean that every bit of the design with all its repeats has to be drawn, without omissions.

The net must be held quite taut and carefully aligned in relation to the pattern so that the cross sides lie straight in a horizontal or vertical direction.

The reference to alignment in the stitch instructions is important in relating the movements of the embroidery thread to the structure of the meshes. The lace can be turned in whatever direction you find easiest to work (though keeping it always face side up), but the path of the thread in passing over or under the twist or cross sides of the net must conform to that shown in the drawing.

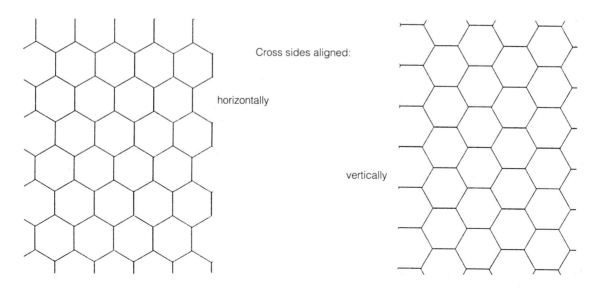

Cross sides aligned:

horizontally

vertically

Threads and needles

A mercerised cotton, such as DMC 30 is convenient for the embroidery. Thicker thread is used for the outline. But there are no categorical imperatives. Classic examples of Limerick lace reveal a broad tolerance of inventiveness.

Any blunt-tipped needle such as a ballpoint, tapestry or crewel can be used. Depending on the mesh size and the form of the stitch, the thickness and length of the needle may need to be varied.

Notes:

1.   In old Limerick laces the embroidery thread was sometimes as thin as, or even thinner than, the double threads which made the mesh sides, thus putting the emphasis on the pattern of holes left between the stitches rather than on the form of the stitches themselves. Use of such thread requires great care - the design all too easily sinks into the background and fails to produce any significant impression. It is however helpful to emphasize the outline of the motifs and the caskets by the use of thick glossy (preferably linen) thread, so that at least there is no mistake about where the stitches are contained.

2.   In the drawings of the various stitches, an attempt has been made to indicate the diameter of the threads in relation to the mesh sides by the use of thicker or thinner lines, but reference to the detailed photographs should clarify this point.

3.   The aim of the drawings is to show as clearly as possible the course to be followed by the embroidery threads. Thus the mesh hole size is much enlarged, and the threads even when double in reality have been represented as thick but single.

4.   Where a needle is shown, no attempt has been made to relate its size to that of the holes. Similarly its thread is shown unrealistically short, so as not to detract from the composition of the stitch itself.

RUNNING THE OUTLINE

The purpose of the outline is to define the shape of the design by transposing it from the inked pattern on to the net. The thread must be thick enough to stand out sharply against the background openwork. Alternatively a thinner thread may be doubled, or even trebled.

Where the thread is single, it can be drawn continuously from a ball or reel. This is also possible if a large enough eyed needle is threaded with two or three strands which are then knotted behind the eye to prevent slippage. The threads are likely to become twisted around each other during working, but this simply makes them look as though they are loosely multiple-plyed.

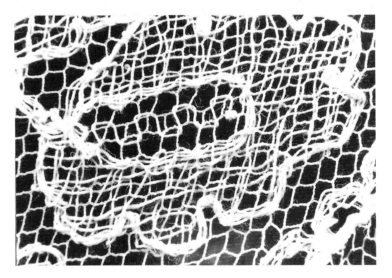

To prevent the reel rolling around, put it inside a polythene bag loosely tied at the top. Or, if a large embroidery frame is used, drive a nail into the wood and fit the central cavity of the reel over it.

For a single thread, take the needle beneath a mesh side and pull the thread through until only a short length remains (x). Hold this end down with the left thumb, take the needle under it, pull the thread through, and tighten it to form a secure knot.

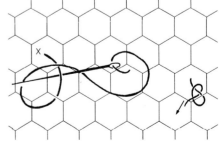

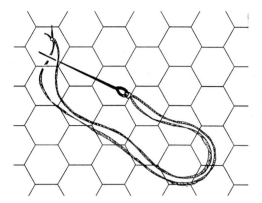

If a length of cut thread is preferred, fold it in two, pass the doubled end through the eye of the needle, and the needle through the loop. Tighten.This keeps the ends equal and the thread from slipping out of the eye. Tie the two free ends together. Take the needle beneath a mesh side, seperate the threads near the knot and slip the needle between them, as shown. Whiskery ends can be trimmed back later.

From this starting point, work carefully around the outline, copying the pattern with precise exactitude, passing the needle in and out of the holes, until you have completed the circuit.

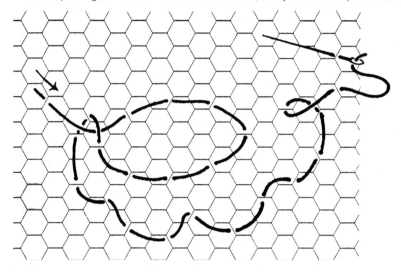

The aesthetic appeal of the lace rests largely on the skill with which the outline is completed. Curves should be smooth and angles sharp. The indents of petals can be indicated by narrow loops, and the limiting sides of the caskets are often worked in continuity with the main shape.

If at any point the thread begins to overtwist, make a slip knot at the ball or reel and allow it to hang and twirl. If the thread becomes badly snarled, cut it, smooth out the twists (or discard a length) and rejoin.

To fasten off the thread, pass it beneath a mesh side, then through the previous stitch, then through loop A, finally tightening it to form a knot.

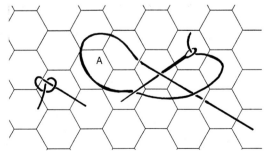

THE SOLID DESIGN AREAS

The outline not only defines the shape of the lace motifs but also forms an anchorage for the embroidery threads.

The stitches which gradually fill in the outline are usually worked in rows, with the thread twining around at either end.

The embroidery thread is used in short lengths, and attached as described for a single-thread outline.

The solid design areas are the denser-appearing areas of the lace. The stitches used are repetitive and closely worked.
There are four main types, named after the embroidery stitches which they resemble:

Running. Darning. Tent. Cross.

Unless otherwise indicated, the cross sides are aligned horizontally.

Running stitch

Row 1.   LR.   Take the needle over and under alternate meshes.
Row 2.   RL.   Repeat in the reverse direction, so that the overs and unders alternate with those of row 1.
Repeat these two rows until the space is filled.

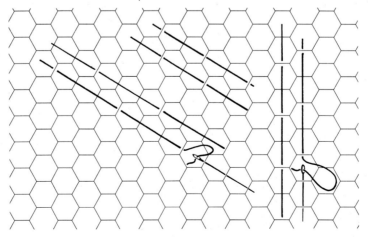

VARIATIONS:

1.   Running stitch may be worked horizontally, vertically or diagonally. In the photograph note how a change in direction of slant is used to give a radiating effect to the petals.

2.   *Taking the rows only part way across the area, and then turning back to leave the bare net, can give a pleasingly dappled effect, as in these horse-chestnut leaves.*

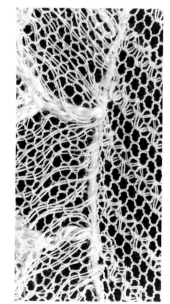

3.   *The number of holes covered by each stitch, and variations in the thickness of the thread, can produce wide deviations in the appearance of simple running stitch areas.*

Darning stitch

This is worked in two sets, the first filling the area before the second is begun. Align the cross sides horizontally.

Set 1. After securing the thread, *stretch it diagonally across the space so that it lies above a line of meshes. At the far side, wind it around the outline to the next diagonal line, and once more stretch it over the net, and secure.
Repeat from * until the whole area is covered with parallel threads, running diagonally.

Set 2. The thread is now taken along lines of meshes slanting in the reverse direction. This time, pass the needle <u>under</u> each mesh side, and <u>over</u> each set 1 thread, in a darning motion.
Continue until the space is filled.

NOTE: the angle at which the two sets of threads cross will depend on the shape of the mesh.

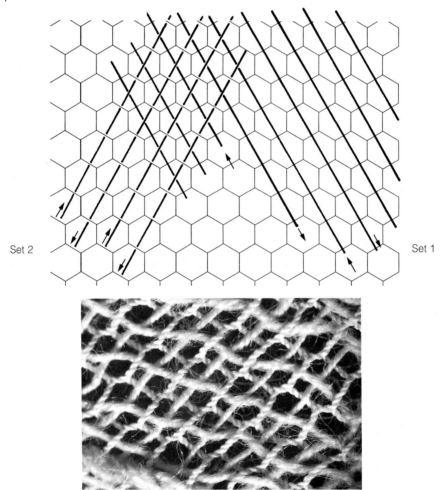

Set 2

Set 1

Tent stitch

Align the cross sides horizontally.
Row 1. Take the needle sideways over 2 twist sides, then under 2 twist sides, as shown. Repeat to the end of the row.
Row 2. Work back again, matching the over-unders with those of row 1, so that all the rows looks alike.

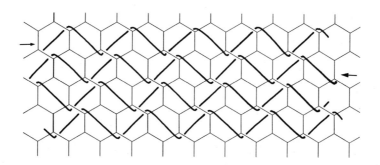

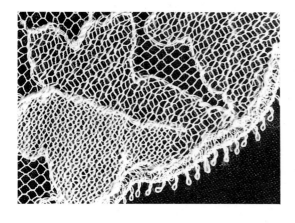
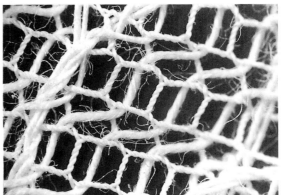

VARIATIONS:
1.   *Work as before, but reverse the over-unders in alternate rows.*

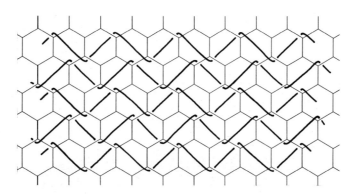

2.   Align the cross sides vertically.

Row 1. Take the needle sideways over 2 cross sides, then downwards under 2 cross sides, working diagonally.

Row 2. Return through the next line of holes, keeping the same over-under sequence and the same thread slope.

NOTE: the diagonals can be aligned either top L-bottom R, or top R-bottom L.

3.   Work as (2) but reverse the over-unders in alternate rows.

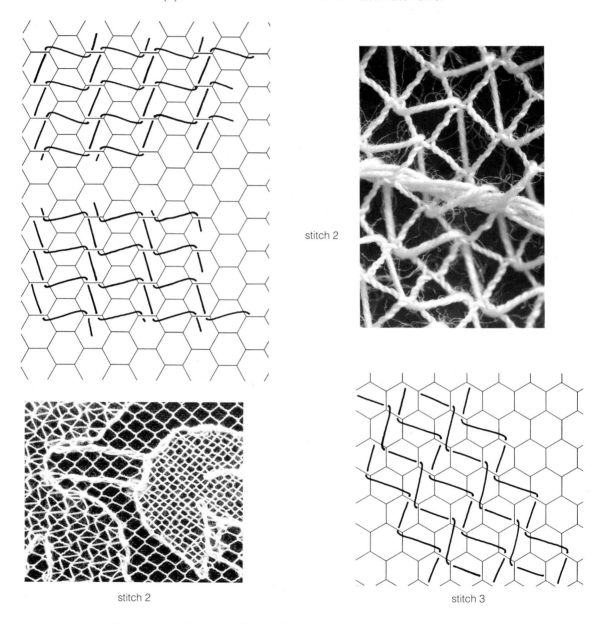

stitch 2

stitch 2

stitch 3

4.   *Tent stitch with empty lines of holes left between the rows produces a lighter effect, and sometimes appears within the caskets.*

Cross stitch

This is like rows 1 and 2 of tent stitch worked along the same line of holes instead of along adjoining ones.
The uppermost thread of each cross passes in the same direction in every mesh, from bottom L to top R, as in embroidery.
Align the cross sides horizontally. Follow the direction indicated by the arrows.

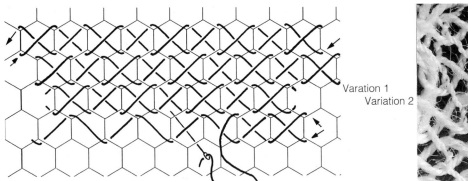

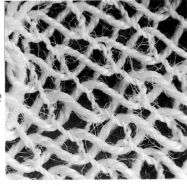

Varation 1
Variation 2

VARIATIONS:

1.   Pack the stitches more closely together so that there is a surface cross over every hole, and the reverse-side crosses are hidden beneath the mesh walls.

2.   Work the rows of cross stitch diagonally.

3.   Leave lines of empty holes between the rows.

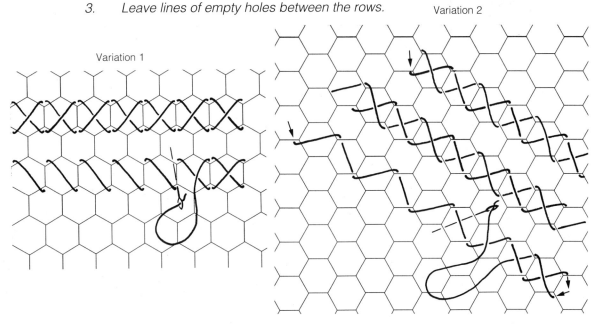

Variation 1

Variation 2

4.   Cross stitch often appears in caskets, not on its own but in association with other stitches.

15

Elaborations of the solid areas: light, shade and three-dimensionality

Attempts at naturalism in design - though deplored by purists as inappropriate to lace - were popular in the last quarter of the 19th century.

Effects of light and shade were achieved quite simply by placing dense and less dense stitches (or sometimes threads) in juxtaposition, on either side of the midrib of a leaf for example, or to distinguish the upper and lower sides of a reflexed petal.

It is sensible to practise the effect before committing it to lace.

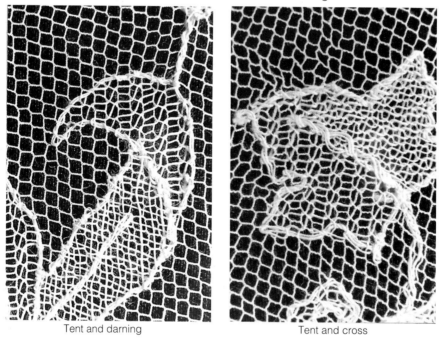

Tent and darning   Tent and cross

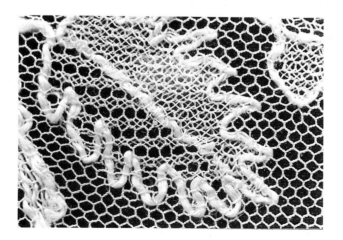

Open and closed
cross stitch
Note also: the
outlines and veins

Veins and holes

The solidity of leaves and petals can be partitioned by thin branching veins. These are often no more than single or double strands of embroidery thread caught down at intervals between the base and tip.

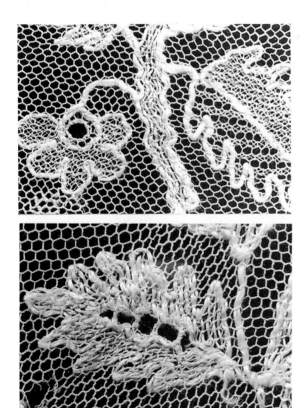

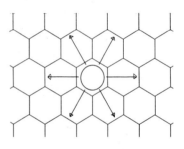

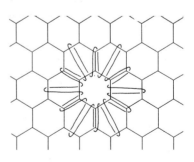

More elaborate veins can be additionally decorative. Holes are enlarged by the use of bodkins, stilettos or borers which burrow downwards to ease the sides of the chosen mesh outwards until the surrounding ring of holes is entirely obscured. The pushed-together sides are tightly overcast to preserve the dilated position. A length of outline cord is then taken around the row of holes, defining the vein.

Practising outlines and solid design area stitches

A series of simple to more complex sketches is given on the next few pages. Even the simplest can produce an attractive effect, such as a flurry of falling leaves filled with different stitches, or combinations of stitches, or directions of stitches, or using different thicknesses of thread.

Trace or photocopy the sketches on to stout paper suitable for use as a pattern, or onto self-adhesive coloured paper which can then be stuck to a card.

Set up the net and support as indicated on p. 5-6.

Nasturtium leaf

Working the outline for the ring of holes. Fill the centre with darning stitch

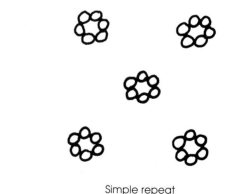

Simple repeat

18

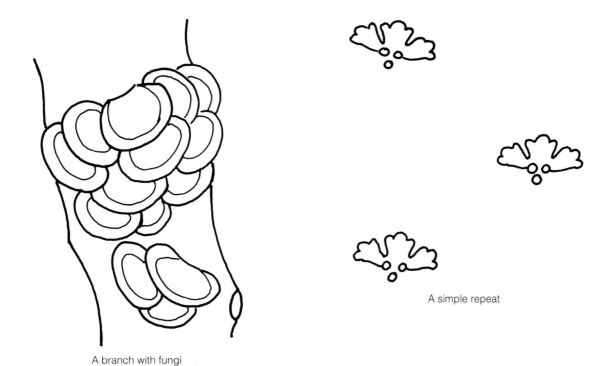

A branch with fungi

A simple repeat

The circles in the net are worked like enlarged holes (p. 17), but without the addition of an outline cord.

Handkerchief border
(after *Weldon's*)

Ivy leaf border

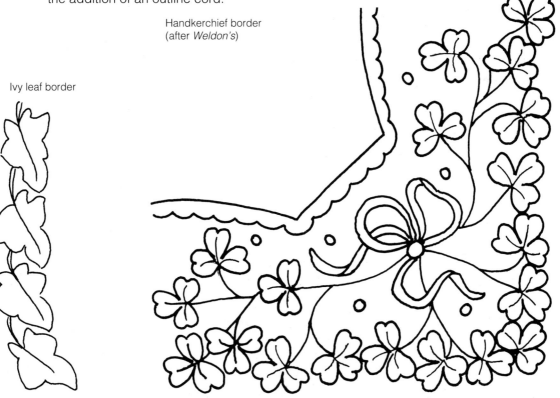

Rose, thistle and shamrock border (after *Weldon's*)

NOTE: If you are new to run embroidery, concentrate on experiment with shapes, and discovery of the effects of stitches. Perfection of working can come later.

Finishing off   Good laces can be made just with solid area stitches, clearly outlined.

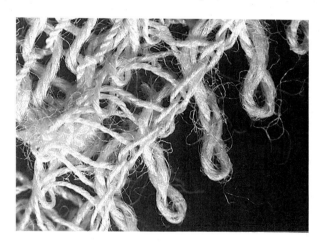

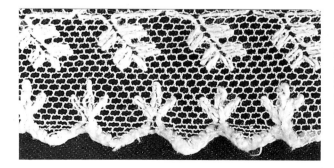

When the work is complete, detach the lace from the pattern by cutting through the tacking stitches at the back. Tidy and strengthen the border by oversewing, buttonhole stitching, or attaching a length of machine picot. Then cut back the net.

THE CASKETS: SOME EXAMPLES

While the stitches of the solid areas are limited in scope and conservative in taste, the fancy stitches which pack the decorative caskets reveal not only a flair for unrestrained inventiveness, but also a sensitive awareness of the subtle changes in appearance which accompany even the most minor variations of stitch spacing and direction of working.

In this section, three pieces of lace have been selected. They will be referred to as:
The Harp Flounce
The Art Nouveau Stole
A Sampler.

THE HARP FLOUNCE

There are two main repeat units, shown in the accompanying photographs.

The Harp Unit

Note: alternate harps along the flounce are reversed

22

The Floral Unit

The outline thread is double throughout.

The photographs show the variation in thread thickness between the outline, the solid design areas, the caskets, and the mesh sides.

The solid design areas are all worked in darning stitch.

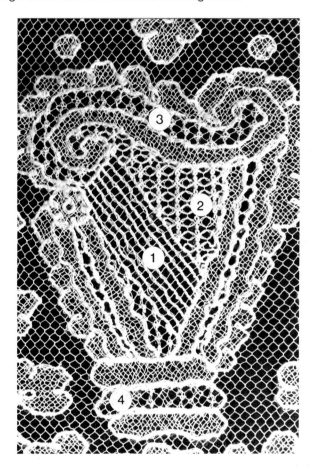

The Harp unit.

In this stylised representation of a harp, the outline thread is curved in ponderous flourishes, to represent the carving of the wood frame.

The fretted pillar and body are pierced by enlarged holes, worked in the same way as the leaf vein (p. 17).

Casket stitch 1 forms the somewhat misplaced strings;

Casket stitch 2 fills the remainder of the central space.

Casket stitch 3 fills the central cavity of the neck, suggesting the brass comb which conceals the mechanism for stopping the strings;

Casket stitch 4 is sandwiched between two solid areas within the pedestal;

Stitch 1. Whipping stitch

Row 1. Work a diagonal row of whipping stitch, using a double thread (this is represented by a single line in the drawing).
Row 2. Work back again along the same track, making sure that the top threads slant consistently in the same direction as those of the first row. A line of twist sides separates one harp string from the next.

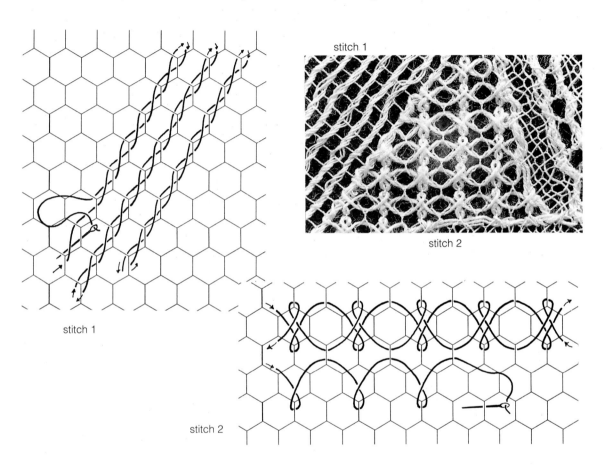

stitch 1

stitch 1

stitch 2

stitch 2

Stitch 2. Detached buttonhole stitch ovals

The ovals are formed by two rows overlapping each other, enclosing a single empty hole.
Row 1. LR. Work dbs loops, taking the needle straight under a cross side above, and backwards under a cross side below. A Z-closure will appear as the thread passes over to the next stitch.
Row 2. At the end of row 1, turn the work around in a clockwise direction so that the right hand side now lies at the left. Work dbs loops in a left-right direction, passing the threads over those of row 1.
Reverse the work to its original position. Repeat these two rows until the casket is filled.

Stitch 3. Crossed figure-of-eight stitch

Follow the course of the embroidery thread shown in the drawing.
At the end of the first row turn the work round so that you again proceed from left to right, though effectively in the reverse direction. The stitches will appear like mirror images.

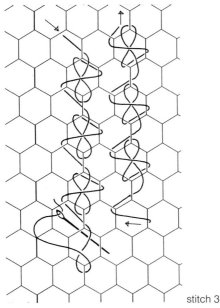

stitch 3

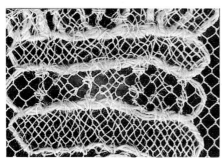

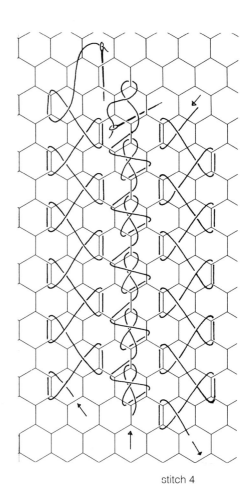

stitch 4

Stitch 4. Herring bone and crossed figure-of-eight stitch

Set 1. *Crossed figure-of-eight.*
Work as described for stitch 1, leaving two lines of empty holes between the stitch rows to accomodate Set 2.
Continue until the casket is filled.

Set 2. *Herringbone stitch.*
Work as shown, taking the needle behind two mesh sides, then over the diagonal thread already laid, to the next position.

Stitch 5

The filling consists of 4-hole blocks of cross stitch linked together and worked diagonally across the casket.
It is found in the large flower (A) to the left of the harp.
Align the cross sides horizontally.
Row 1. Follow the course of the arrows.
Leave a line of holes.
Row 2. Turn the lace round and work back, still proceeding LR. The overs and unders of the thread crossings will now appear reversed.
Note also the decorative veining which alleviates the blandness of the darning stitch petals.

Detail of stitch 5 from flower (A)

27

Stitch 6.

Large flower (B) to the right of the harp also encloses a single casket stitch, composed here of alternating rows of tent stitch and satin stitch worked diagonally from top L to bottom R.

Set 1. Tent stitch. Take the thread horizontally over 2 cross sides, then across the reverse side to the mid-one below. Repeat to the end of the row.
The rows are placed 3 holes apart, and the thread movements in each row are identical. Continue until the casket is filled.

Set 2. Satin Stitch. Work in the mid-line of holes left between the rows of Set 1.
Take the thread twice around the twist sides of mesh (a), then carry it across the reverse side to the exit.
Go over the next cross side, and under the following one. Enter mesh (b), and repeat. The thread movements in each row are identical.

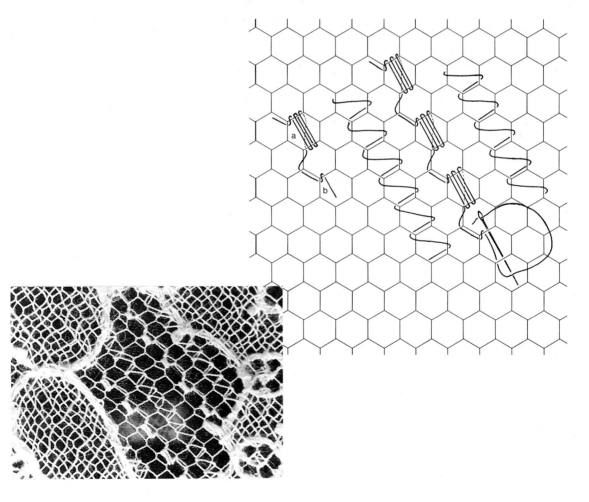

28

Stitch 7. Cobweb stitch

This lies in the small flower between the harp and the ear of wheat.
Align the cross sides horizontally.
Elongate alternate holes (marked o) in a horizontal direction. Work the
cobweb stitches in paired rows, arranging them to mirror-image each
other.

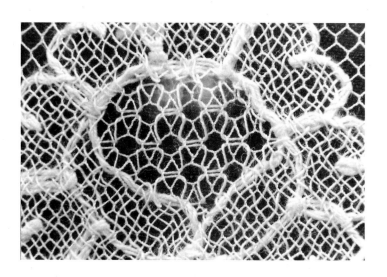

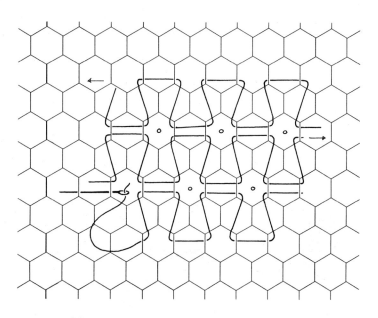

29

The Floral unit.

This area of the design introduces two new stitches:

Stitch 8. Dbs ovals and cross stitch

This is a variation of stitch 2, with rows of cross stitch (in fine thread) alternating with the rows of ovals (in thick thread).

Set 1. Ovals: work as stitch 4, leaving an empty line of holes between each row of stitches. The over-unders of the embroidery thread are identical in every row, but note that the stitches themselves alternate in position.

Set 2. Cross stitch: work a row of cross stitch in every line of holes left between the rows of ovals.
The slant of the overlying stitches is reversed in successive rows, and it may be found helpful to turn the lace round as described in stitch 2 and 3 (p. 25, 26).

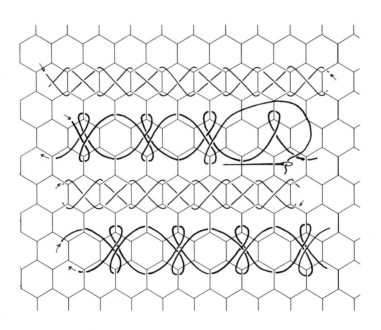

Stitch 9. Figure-of-eight and cobweb stitch

Work horizontally.

Set 1. The figure-of-eight stitches are worked first, using an embroidery thread scarcely thicker than the mesh sides, but additional weight is added by taking the thread twice around the course before passing on to the next position. In the drawing, single threads only have been shown for the sake of clarity.
Take the needle over the twist sides and under the cross sides as indicated by the arrows. The upper and lower figures are all worked in a single row.
Turn the work round between rows to achieve a mirror-image effect.

Set 2. When the casket has been filled with Set 1 stitches, return to the beginning and work the cobweb stitches. Their horizontal sides pass over the figure-of-eights, and their sloping sides below the meshes.

NOTE: *In the drawing, Sets 1 and 2 are shown separately at the R and L sides, before being superimposed.*

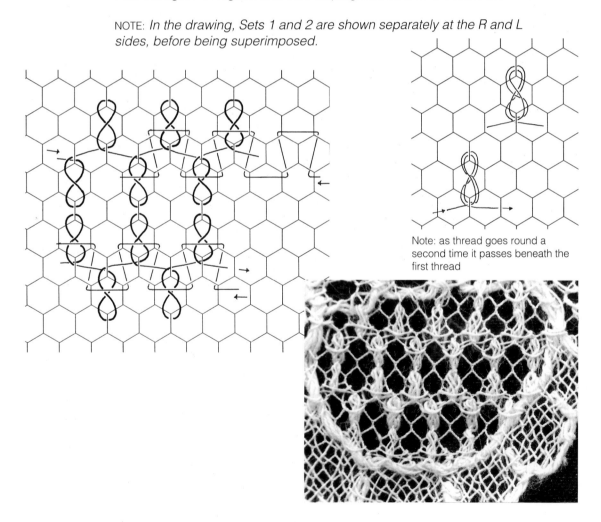

Note: as thread goes round a second time it passes beneath the first thread

31

The solid design areas are worked in darning stitch (p. 12).

The isolated holes scattered through the net are made as described on p. 17, though without the outline cord. They are badly constructed and may be a later addition.

The outline cord is double. It appears at times to be whipped through the meshes, rather than run.

The embroidery threads are the same thickness as the mesh sides.

Stitch 1. Overlapping cobweb stitch

Align the cross sides vertically.

The cobweb stitches are arranged so that the horizontal threads of consecutive rows overlap, forming a narrow elipse. At the same time they pull on the intermediate holes (marked o), distending them sideways. This distortion can be assisted by a bodkin if necessary.

Row 1. Work cobweb stitch horizontally, passing the top and bottom threads <u>over</u> the cross sides.

Row 2. Work back as indicated by the arrows, passing the top and bottom threads <u>under</u> the cross sides.

Repeat these two rows until the casket is filled.

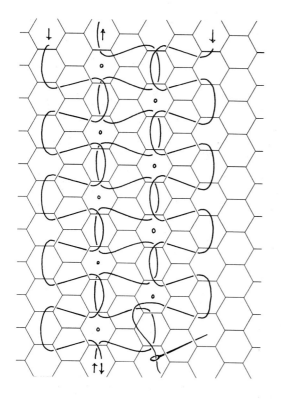

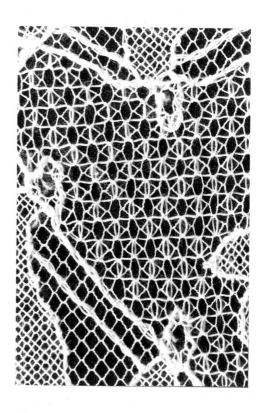

This motif, filled with casket stitches 1 and 3, would make an attractive border.

Stitch 2. Tent stitch, a variation

Align the cross sides vertically. Work the rows of tent stitch diagonally from top L to bottom R.
After every fourth row move the stitches along 1 mesh so that their alignment is thrown out.

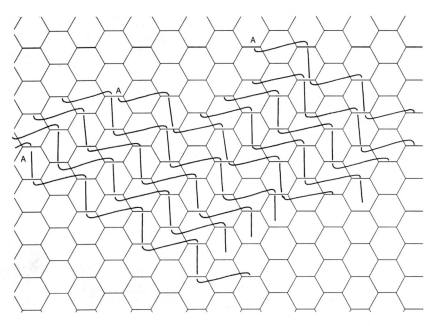

Stitch 3.

This is a single row of cossed figure-of-eight stitches, worked as in the Harp Flounce, stitch 4 (p. 26).

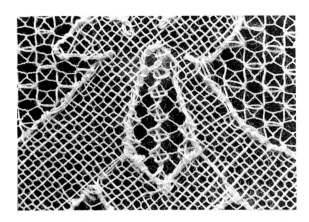

Stitch 4. Crossed figure-of-eight stitch reversed

This is the same as stitch 3, except that there are a number of rows, the cross sides are aligned vertically, the rows are worked horizonatlly, and what appears on the face of the net is in fact the back of the stitch as normally worked.
The stitches alternate with each other in successive rows, while their thread movements are mirror-imaged.

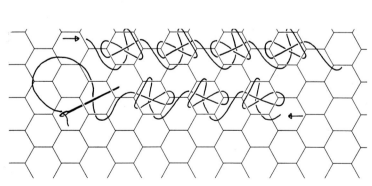

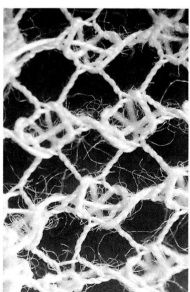

Stitch 5. Tent stitch diamonds with satin stitch crosses.

Align the cross sides vertically.

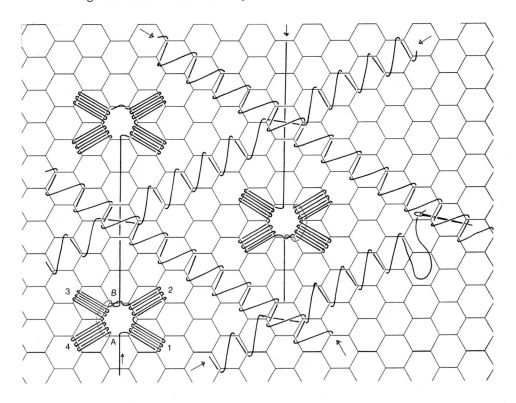

Set 1. *Work diagonal rows of close tent stitching from bottom L to top R across the casket, spacing the rows 5 holes apart, as shown in the drawing.*

Set 2. *Work diagonal rows of tent stitch from bottom R to top L so that they intersect with set 1 forming a trellis-work of diamonds each containing 25 holes. Simplify the crossing points by making a larger stitch beneath set 1 (note the position of the needle).*
Continue until the casket is filled.

Set 3.   Row 1. LR. *Enter at A and *work 3 satin stitches over each of the meshes 1, 2, 3, 4, proceeding in an anti-clockwise direction.*
Take the embroidery thread through the back of blocks 4 and 3, to B.
Carry it across 5 meshes to the centre hole of the next diamond, passing beneath the trellis-work intersection. Repeat from * to the far side of the casket.
        Row 2. *Turn the work round,and work back through the next set of tent stitch diamonds, again in a LR direction.*
Continue in this way until all the crosses are worked.

WORKING A SAMPLER

The photograph shows the complete design from which the detail on p.2 was taken.

Note how the heavy run stitch of the solid areas provides a foil for the delicate variety of casket stitches, and how changes in direction of the casket stitches themselves give vitality and interest to the whole.

The stitches found in the original lace are described and illustrated on the following pages. You can use these, or your own initiative, to fill in the various enclosures, blending and contrasting the stitches with an eye to harmony - like painting a patchwork of varied colours.

R = run

T = tent

C = cross

Unmarked spaces are
filled with run stitches

Stitch 1. Cobweb stitch.

Enlarge alternate holes (marked O) along two diagonal lines as shown.
*Link the holes by cobweb stitch.
Enlarge a further line of holes, and repeat from * until the casket is filled.
A thin embroidery thread gives equal weight to the mesh sides, so that,
in the final impression, the casket appears to be filled with tiny rosettes
nestling around cavities (see photo).

NOTE: *In the central leaf, the stitches are arranged in vertical rows.*

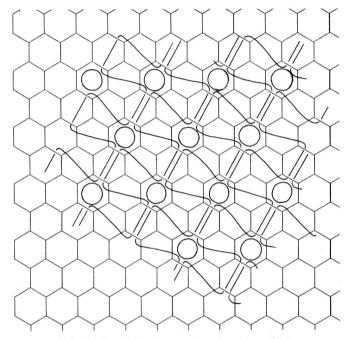

Stitch 2. Reinforced cobweb stitch.

Work cobweb stitches in a horizontal direction, but instead of simply
passing the straight side beneath a mesh, take it twice around it, in the
manner of satin stitch.
Repeat until the casket is filled.

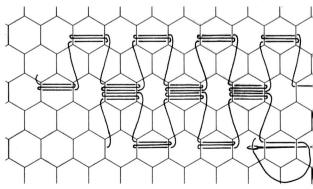

Stitch 3. Cross stitch and whip stitch.

Align the cross sides vertically.
Row 1. LR. Work along a diagonal path, whipping the embroidery thread over the twist sides.
Leave a line of holes.
Rows 2 and 3. RL and LR. Work a row of cross stitch.
Leave a line of holes.
Row 4. RL. Work as row 1, but slanting the upper stroke in the reverse direction.
Leave a line of holes.
Rows 5 and 6. LR and RL. Work as rows 2 and 3, but slanting the upper stroke in the reverse direction.
Repeat these 6 rows until the casket is filled.

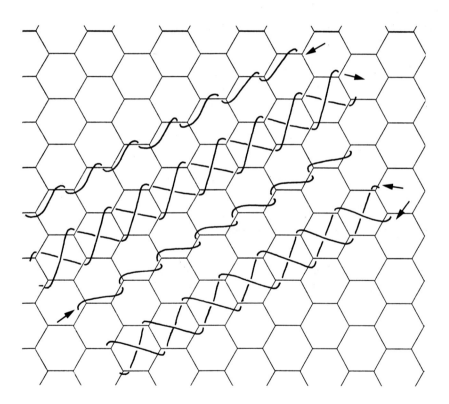

Stitch 4. Rows of extended tent stitch alternate with rows of whip stitch, spaced one line of holes apart.

Follow the overs and unders of the embroidery thread indicated in the line drawing.
The tent stitch rows can be worked as a Set, followed by all the whip stitch rows. Or, if preferred, they can be worked in alternation, LR rows tent stitch, and RL rows whip stitch.

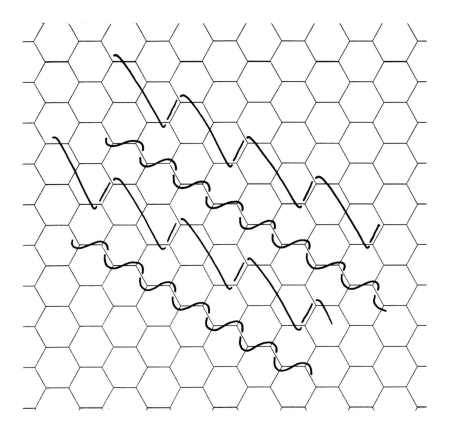

Stitch 5. Tent stitch trellis with satin stitch spots.

Set 1. *Construct a tent stitch trellis as in the Art Nouveau Stole st.5 (p.37), again making the diamonds 3 holes across.*

Set 2. *Work 4 satin stitches around the central hole of each trellis diamond. Link the spots of adjacent units by whipping the embroidery thread along the mesh sides, passing beneath the intersections of the trellis.*

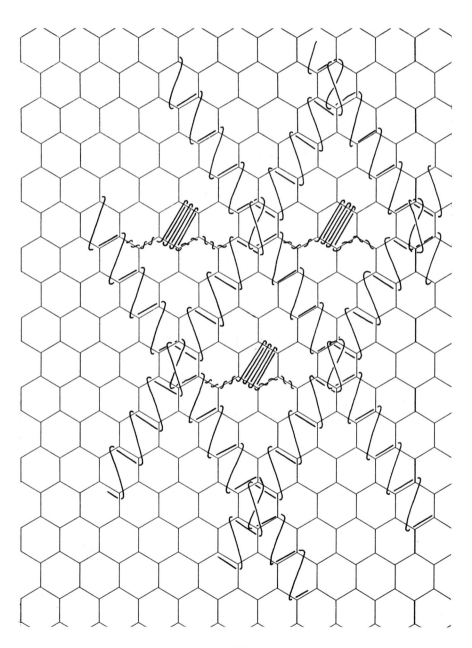

Stitch 6. Tent stitch trellis with needle-woven spots.

Set 1. *Construct a tent stitch trellis, spacing the rows three holes apart. In this example, the stitches are slightly more reflexed than in st.5.*

Set 2. *In the centre hole of each unit, work a tight needle-woven spot, using slightly thicker thread to make a very solid knob.*

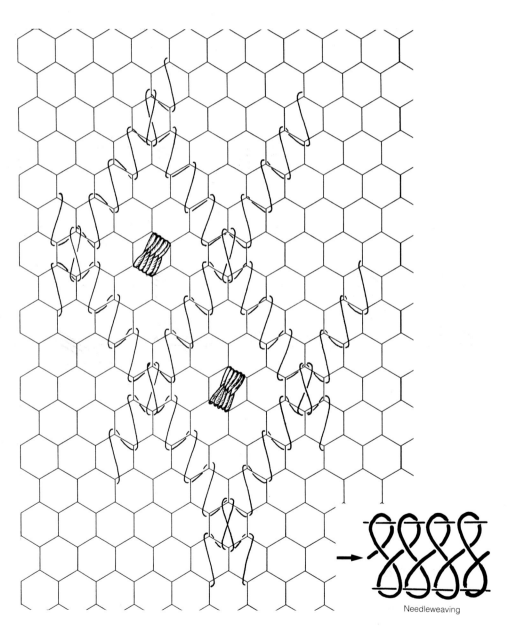

Needleweaving

44

Stitch 7. A trellis of run stitches centred with satin stitch flowers.

Set 1. *Using thick thread, work 3 rows of run stitch through a single diagonal line of holes, passing from top L to bottom R. Leave 5 lines of holes, and repeat until the casket is filled.*

Set 2. *Work similar diagonals along a top R-bottom L axis. At the intersections, pass the threads under the stitches of set 1 without attempting to run them through the already filled holes.*

Set 3. *Using a finer thread, work 6-petalled satin stitch flowers around the central hole of each trellis diamond. The flowers are not linked together. Instead, leave the thread hanging at the back to be sewn in later.*

Stitch 8. Alternating rows of tent stitch and satin stitch.

See Harp Flounce st.6 (p.28).

DEFINITIONS

alignment - arranging the meshes of a net so that their cross sides are straight on to the design in either a vertical or a horizontal direction.

bobbinet - a machine net, invented in 1808, and made by twisting warp and bobbin threads around each other at the sides (twist sides), and crossing them at the top and bottom of each mesh (cross sides). The bobbin threads run diagonally (the net is traversed).

bodkin, borer, stiletto - a tapering implement of bone, wood or metal, used to enlarge holes in a net or loosely woven fabric.

caskets (casques) - enclosures destined to be filled with decorative stitches.

detached buttonhole stitch (dbs) - a stitch made with a single thread manipulated to form rows of interlocking loops. Commonly found in the solid design areas of needle laces.

Limerick lace - techniques of hand embroidery on machine net, originating in the city of Limerick, but becoming widespread.

outline - a thread which fixes the shape of the design areas and forms an anchorage for the later-added stitches.

Raschel net - machine net made by a warp-knitting process.

round net - bobbinet with all sides of its hexagonal meshes equal in length.

run lace - embroidery of a machine net by taking the needle and thread alternately over and under the mesh sides.

solid areas - densely worked areas intended to dominate the design.

sq   with 4 long twist sides and 2 very short cross sides.